Just for You

Edited by Rachael Radford

First published in Great Britain in 2002 by
POETRY NOW
Remus House,
Coltsfoot Drive,
Peterborough, PE2 9JX
Telephone (01733) 898101
Fax (01733) 313524

HB ISBN 0 75434 339 1
SB ISBN 0 75434 340 5

Foreword

The modern world is often seen as fast-moving, hectic and complicated, with little or no time to sit back, take a deep breath and remember the people who have helped shape our lives. *Just For You* defies this, it demands that you take the time to read the multitude of poems that have been chosen to entertain and inspire.

The poets included in this book have their own message of love and thanks to give, their own story or anecdote to share, their own chosen language and poetic form. It is the variety of content and style which is bound to appeal to all poetry enthusiasts for years to come.

Rachael Radford
Editor

Our English Rose
On Page 93
Written by :-
Susan Carole Roberts

Contents

The Short Life Of Grace Darling	R T Owen	10
Nana Said	Elaine Edgar	11
Dreams Part 4 - 'The Final Dream'	Chris Barber	12
Miriam The Gipsy Girl	Thomas Hull	13
Rachel	Ted Medler	14
For Joshua	Sheila Seabourne	15
Christmas Dreaming	Anita Richards	16
My Father	Annette Murphy	17
Philip William	Nanny Smith	18
My Special Friend	J Moore	20
So Long My Friend	Stephen A Owen	21
Innocent Feeling	Hacene Rahnouni	22
Cecil Frances Alexander	Georgina Johnston	23
Losing Pauline	Felicite R Gill	24
A Princess	Karen Burke	25
Nanny Lee	Mark Page	26
My Uncle Theodore	Hilda Grace Hutchin	27
1887	Allan Bula	28
Angel Of The Light	Valerie Ann Knight	29
Happiness	Victoria Churcher	30
Mother	Angela Cheyne	31
Remembering You On Father's Day	Lynn Edwards	32
The Golden Wedding Day	Isobel Guthrie	33
Dreamtime	John K Coleridge	34
Lady Of Gathered Morning	George Coombs	35
Ralf	Olive Hudson	36
The Cowshed	Rona Laycock	37
Golden Time	D M Norris	38
The Welcome Thief	Sandra Holden	39
Morag	Neil Halliday	40
Bruv	E A Triggs	41
Splendour Of The Morn	Séamas M Ó Dálaigh	42
Daisy	A J Lowe	43
Sonnet To An Aged Love	Jack Scrafton	44
The Lover's Song	Myra Bowen	45
Patricia	W Ballantyne Scott	46

Small Is Beautiful	Kevin J Hodge	47
You	Sarah Hardy	48
My Little Devil And Angel	Parveen K Saini	49
My Rock	Marian Curtis-Jones	50
Mother	Bakewell Burt	51
Our Time	B J Polhill	52
Alchemy	Bernard Brown	53
A Poem For You	Nia Michael	54
Where Were You?	Jessie Baxter	55
The Man Who Shot An Albatross	Andrew Farmer	56
Love Shared, Love Lost	Eleanor Margaret Brooks	57
He Cares	Louise White	58
Roydon	Janine Vallor	59
For Nathan	David W Lankshear	60
Just Waiting	Clive Cornwall	61
To G	Mary Hughes	62
Adele	John Foster	63
Mater	Simon Knight	64
None Other	Michael Ashcroft	65
Missing You, Julie Savage	Maria Bradley	66
Mary	E Backham	67
40 Years Of Love	David G Bromage	68
The Silent Poem	Joan Hands	69
Roger And Jane Wedding Day 2002	Roger Brooks	70
My Special Friend	Patricia M Farbrother	71
A Symphony In Grey	M E Vanderwulp	72
A Poem For Nan	Marilyn Wellman	73
Thank You Jesus	Samantha Drewry	74
What Are Mams And Dads?	F J Lawton	76
The Package	Kevin Rolfe	77
Just One More Spoonful	Yvonne Lane	78
A Mother's Recipe	Isabel Morgan	80
I Miss You	Lydia Moore	81
For Janet	Brigitta D'Arcy	82
Farewell Princess	Terry Daley	83
A Daughter	Barbara Brown	84
Deep And Darker Brown	Edward Fursdon	85
To Gina	Chris Gutteridge	86
My Dad, My Hero	Pat Munzer	87

Diana	Frederica Greenway	88
Man Of Years	Marshal Green	89
The Death Of Princess Margaret	J Nicoll	90
Margaret Rose	Isabella F Veitch	91
A Beautiful Lady	Margaret Stumpp	92
Our English Rose	Susan Carole Roberts	93
Christine	Michelle Knight	94
Fly Like A Bird	Marian Reid	95
Princess Diana (1961-1997)	Josie May Hodges	96
A Soul Concern	Rachel Taylor	97
Dear Sister	M Ackroyd	98
Mum	Neil Stirk	99
Theresa - A Memory	Brian L Porter	100
Alexandra	A Moore	101
Dad	Laura O'Rourke	102
Someone Much Loved	Burgess J Barrow	103
Mei Tak	Mei Yuk Wong	104
Dunkirk - The Final Tribute	A Yap-Morris	105
Smile	Helen Owen	106
Mary's Love	John Crowe	107
Just An Ordinary Afternoon	Deborah Grimwade	108
Elizabeth Our Queen	Wendy Le Maitre	110
Untitled	Colin Drummond	111
Peter	Sue Trickey	112
The Soldiers Of The Queen	Tony Dixon	114
Our Grandchildren	Ruth Baker	115
A Tribute To Kevin . . .	Angela Tsang	116
My Two Angels Of Beauty	Donald John Tye	117
To Elizabeth From Her Grandmother	B E	118
You Mean The World To Me	Lindsey Hood	119

The Poems

The Short Life Of Grace Darling

Grace Darling was a lighthouse keeper's daughter
The lass who became a life saving legend
They rowed in a small boat in dreadful weather
That is Grace and her father, they rowed it seems without an end.
They went to help survivors of a wreck named 'Forfar Shire'
They assisted five of the survivors from the reef
The wind was blowing roughly and the rain in the air.
This young woman was only twenty-three when she did this deed.
Once the first party was safe in Longstone light
William Darling and two of the rescued crew went back
To fetch the persons still alive on the wreck's site.
Lives were saved and article retrieved time to relax
They found nine persons still alive on the wreck.
Grace Darling was already being hailed as a heroine
Those souls lost, and those were off the wreck deck
William Darling and his daughter thought it hard going.
Grace was born in the cottage, her grandfather's home
In 1815 the date was the 24th November.
One can see even today Grace Darling's tomb
She died a young woman of twenty-seven
Oh, the bravery of grace Darling.

R T Owen

Nana Said

Nana said, 'Eat up your breakfast there's a good girl'
As I frantically disentangle a matted up curl that's escaped
From my pigtail and draped in the milk.

The sunlight is pouring in through the open door
Hovering around like torchlight beams scouring the floor.
'Oh Nana can I leave it please?' - I do so long to scamper off
And climb up some trees.

'You eat up your breakfast first, then we'll see' -
'But the milk's off Nana,' I plea.
'Oh no - I am not falling for that one Hun.
It's fresh this very morning so no fear of that!'
'But it's warm Nana and it tastes funny,' - oh drat!

'Eat up or else,' my nana chides, but my mind is already
Wandering to that outdoor slide.
Well, just a plank of wood really sloping down from the seat
And the splinters I'd encountered ooh, but I would never be beat.

Reluctantly I gobble up every last flake then dash off to dare
Another adventure as I leave chaos in my wake.
Nana is firmly standing her ground
Shaking her head and sighing aloud
'What will I do with you Hun?' she says.
Oh deary me, I can tell she is miffed
'But oh Nana, you know how I hate warm milk
On my cornflakes,' I sniff!

Elaine Edgar

Dreams Part 4 - 'The Final Dream'

(Dedicated to Sue Nicholson)

Now that the dreams have finally gone
I have lost you forever,
The dreams of you have left me
How do I cope without you?

There'll be no more kissing your sweet lips
And no more touching your smooth skin,
I remember the final dream
When you cried and said, 'Goodbye'.

You kissed me gently
And you held me in your arms,
Your heart was beating with mine
As you said, 'I love you'.

Now that the dreams are over
I will see my dream girl no more,
Your eyes will never sparkle again
And now all I will feel is pain.

Chris Barber

Miriam The Gipsy Girl

Miriam the gipsy girl with tambourine in hand
You danced so seductively upon the yellow sand.
Wearing a black dress with roses round your neck
Your dark eyes brooding with the spirit of a fire
Wild and not tame burning with earthly desire.
I held her in my arms charmed by her feminine grace
Touched by the love and smile on her face.
When we two virgins kissed, oh what bliss.
It tasted so sweet, like red wine crushed from the grape.
You flamed like a comet across the sky within my mind
I had seen for the first time a truly heavenly sign.
Then playfully you read my palm
And with a prophet's searching gaze
You played your part speaking sincerely from the heart.
Sadness covered your beautiful face
And a single tear fell from your black velvet eyes.
You said with solemn voice
Angels stand guard around you
Until the appointed hour.
Then you will be crushed for love's sake
In the battle between the powers.
Then you smiled so sweetly and looked into my eyes
And I was in love for the very first time.

Thomas Hull

Rachel

(For Rachel - A friend)

I'm a woman.
I'm Rachel. I'm unique.
There has never been before
And never will be again
. . . another me.
I'm here because I'm a child of God.
I'm beautiful.
I'm rich because I'm loved.
No one has any rights over me.
I'm free. I'm single.
I can do anything I want
As long as I don't hurt anyone
. . . those that I love,
Or that love me.
I'm able to move mountains
. . . yet there is a side of me
That is as fragile as
The wings of a butterfly.
I can be hurt. I can cry
. . . But no man will ever
Totally enslave me.
For I am Rachel!

Ted Medler

For Joshua

Beyond the gate a whole new world awaits,
But he is only two, must stand and stare.
Watch through wooden slats, his mate,
Free at five years, to cycle round that square.
He will wait all his life to catch him up.
Just three steps behind, but he will not know,
Not until middle age and with a glow,
      Remember,
Through a crack of memory,
Two inches by four,
Sight of freedom
Through a bolted garden door.

Sheila Seabourne

Christmas Dreaming

He is my son
third from the left,
handsome with
deep brown eyes
and jet-black hair.
His fine fingers
turn the pages
of my heart.

He reminds me
of his father.
He sings loud and clear,
as carols echo the air.
In the choir stalls at King's,
the choirboy, third from the left
he - he is my son . . . for a moment -
a brief Christmas dream moment.

For in this lifetime, unborn was my son . . .

Anita Richards

My Father

I knew a man long ago,
Who said he was my father.
He was big and strong.
Feared nothing but death.

He could be impatient at times,
Or even fearsome when I'd done wrong.
But mostly, he was gentle and kind.
He enveloped me with love.

When I was young, he knew everything,
But as I grew older, for a while, I knew all.
The tables turned again as I matured,
And we shared ideas, learnt from each other.

He taught me life's important rules.
By showing love, how to love,
By trusting, how to trust,
By giving respect, how to respect.

Then one day, the news he feared.
An evil cancer was squeezing the breath from his lungs.
Time was short; his clock was ticking ever faster.
But he'd had time to love me unconditionally.

As I watched my father diminish,
I saw an inner calmness push through.
Every breath seized with such effort,
Then, a strange stillness that belied his death.

I knew that the death he once feared,
Became his longing.
The evil didn't win.
My father, to a new life, just gave in.

Annette Murphy

Philip William

Who can read far into the night?
Who can write, 'til his heart takes flight?
Who can multiply, making six become sixty?
My grandson . . . Philip William!

Who can run with speed of a deer?
Who deftly swims without any fear?
Who wears a white suit, and kicks his legs in the air?
My grandson . . . Philip William!

Who paints pictures of Darth Maul
Who puts them up on his bedroom wall?
Who'll jump out of his skin, should they fall?
My grandson . . . Philip William!

Who goes to Cubs, in his jumper so smart?
Who listens quietly, as their words they impart?
Who knows a 'Pip' is really (shsh) a fart!
My grandson . . . Philip William!

Who rises early (about half-past six)?
Who turns on the 'telly', and gets up to his tricks?
Who's got one foot bigger than t'uther?
My grandson . . . Philip William!

Who loves surprises, both giving and receiving?
Who'll give you a hug, if he sees you grieving?
Who's not quite sure if he likes the teasing?
My grandson . . . Philip William!

Who's got a smashin' mum and dad?
Whose grandad would give him the shirt off his back?
Who likes cockles and Chinese seaweed?
My grandson . . . Philip William!

Who has promised me a poem to stick on my wall?
Who will grow up to be six feet tall?
Who will help you up - should you fall?
My grandson . . . Philip William!

Who now bids you 'Sweet dreams' and may God bless and keep you
Safe from all harm, wrapped in goodness and light?
Who knows the answer to all of these questions?
Philip William!

Nanny Smith

My Special Friend

My friend I will never forget you
Wherever I go I will always see you.
We went to school together
And friends we stayed forever.
Our families grew up, we kept in touch
I needed someone to lean on, you were there
And now you are gone, you are in my prayer.
I feel you with me all the while
I can still see your happy smile.
In this life I miss you
In the next life I will see you
And together we will always be friends.

J Moore

So Long My Friend

(Dedicated to my special dog Roxie, from Karen)

Sorry you had to go this way
I wish you didn't have to
I wish you could stay.
I'm gonna miss you that's for sure
What more can I give you?
Wish I could give you more.
I have done all that I can to try to understand
But I know it is nearly time for you to go
Hey baby I'm gonna really miss you.

So my friend please don't cry
In my heart you will be by my side
We get one chance in this meaning of life
Do not know why you had to die.

It's three in the morning, didn't get any sleep last night
Kept stroking your face and wondering why
You look so good cannot believe it's true
You've only just left me, tell me what am I gonna do?
I held your paw, wish you could've let me know
Before the angels took you
How did they know?
We get one chance in this cruel, cruel life
Promised I'd care for you right through your life
Just put your collar and tag, laid it on your bed
Thought of the nice memories
And the good times we had.

Goodbye my friend you don't mind if I cry
Sitting here with your toys, I have tears in my eyes,
You look so peaceful, a relieved look on your face
The pain has gone
Have fun in your new place.

Stephen A Owen

Innocent Feeling

(Especially to Diana)

Your nice smile
attracts me towards you
without any words
I'm still looking to you
why I missed the words
when I saw you?
I spent the night dreaming of you
I spent the night running after you.
If our hearts could be linked
I'd throw mine
just to spend a moment with you.
Your nice smile
attracts me towards you
without any words
without any words
I'm still looking to you.

Hacene Rahnouni

22

Cecil Frances Alexander

No plaque to mark her birthplace,
no sainthood she was given.
The little girl from Dublin
so famous would become.

Around the pleasant woods she roamed,
her mind was filled with awe.
She recognised the Great Creator,
in everything she saw.

Her kindly deeds were known around,
from Killeter to Strabane.
Fahan and the Maiden City,
her good works did abound.

In sunshine, showers of rain or hail,
she travelled near and far.
To tend the sick and dying, too
and show God's love and care.

Her words are sung in Ireland,
In far off lands as well.
'There is a Green Hill Far Away'
inspired us near and far.

Lord let us follow in her steps,
always conscious of God's love.
Give us faith and courage that
we may cast all our care on you.

No plaque to mark her birthplace,
no sainthood she was given.
Her name is held in reverence,
and hallowed will remain.

Georgina Johnston

Losing Pauline

She was warm and vibrant up till then
yet suddenly so swiftly gone.
We heard the news at break of day
of this wicked dreadful wrong,
how hard to try and still be strong.

Her body cold, her face wax white
no longer mine to touch or hold,
though surely that's a mother's right
to comfort her and hold her tight
on that awesome viewing night?

Her wet lank hair lay round her head
while she rested on a metal bed.
Though life could do her no more harm
I longed to hold her in my arms
and try to ease her fears and qualms.

Her worries ceased, her cares dispelled,
though heavy burdened we move on,
our lives don't end with her life felled.
Her children renew her forty years
and doing so erase and ease our tears.

Felicite R Gill

A Princess

As a princess you brought happiness,
Very formal yet so normal,
A beautifulness yet a shyness that surrounds you
You cared for the old and young,
All countries and nations around the world.

Once again God sent us an angel,
And once again we let him down,
You never ever wore a crown
And never did you frown.
Yet alone tears you shed
And your loneliness you did hide.
To greet us with your impish smile
Our love and thoughtfulness,
I cut a pack of cards and what did I see?
The Queen of Hearts looking at me.

Karen Burke

Nanny Lee

(Dedicated to my Nan Lee)

At the grand old age of 81
The star in my sky
So brightly she has shone
Her fighting spirit
And burning desire
The one I love
And will always admire
Her welcoming smile
Such a delight
The sun in my life
Giving me light
Her beautiful face
And gave up she never
Her place in my heaven
For ever and ever

Mark Page

My Uncle Theodore

My uncle was called Theodore
Never saw him, never met him,
Perished in the Great War long ago,
Only seventeen and a half.

Merchant Navy boy, well liked, well loved,
Even asked my mother once, 'Florrie are you walking out?'
'Yes,' she replied, 'I'm walking out with Fred,'
Theodore was an altar boy at St Andrew's Church,
Came from Stockwell, London.

Grandmama received the telegram one day, black edged,
Chief Petty Officer tried to save his life on the
SS Belgian Prince.
As his life slowly ebbed away,
He said, 'Don't weep for me, for I'm in the hands of God now.'

The Belgian Prince was torpedoed off the cost of
Newport, Rhode Island, USA by the Russian Navy, I believe,
I should like to think his body lies in calm waters,
And maybe it's a pretty place!

Special boy you were not meant to live to be old,
I'm only your niece, but I have your medals now.

And on the Stockwell War Memorial,
Your name still stands with the other boys,
Dear Theodore, a great name of the sea,
You shall not be forgotten.

Hilda Grace Hutchin

1887

1887 was the year when
Queen Victoria's golden jubilee was
Held and 50 years of service crowned with
Celebrations all through festive Britain.

Happy fam'ly life and sympathy with
Simple people; tragic widowhood and
Touching courage were rewarded all at
Once with drums and trumpets, crowds and cheering.

Britain's living symbol lasted 13
Years more till her death at over 80,
Three years after diamond jubilations.
She remains our longest-reigning monarch.

But in stirring '87 came the
Hazard threat'ning all then-current figures,
Whether living, dying, battling, being
Executed or assassinated.

Will McGonagall was this risk to all who
Earned his notice. Thus Queen Vicky did not
Dodge the words below as loyal homage
William penned for half a cent'ry's duty:

'Victoria is a good queen, which all her subjects know,
And for that may God protect her from every foe;
May He be as a hedge around her as He's been all along,
And let her live and die in peace - is the end of my song.'

Allan Bula

Angel Of The Light

(Ode to Auntie Aud)

From whence you came, you go,
Lighting the path;
Your light has touched so many lives
With unconditional love.
Your joy of living, and your laugh
Have brightened many hours.

Your strength has been a strength for others,
A rock to lean upon;
Your life has been a message,
A lesson for us all;
You've loved us, Angel of the Light,
And we have loved you too.

The place you go is full of light
For you to drink your fill,
And send it out revitalised
For all who need to see.
Your power will get greater,
Your love will build yet more,
To show the ones that follow,
The miracle in store.

You will be inspiration,
You will be strength to grow,
You will be joy of living,
And love of things we know.
From where you are, you'll guide us,
Your smile will light the track,
Your arms will be around us
To tell us you'll be back.

We love you.

Valerie Ann Knight

Happiness

H	orrible days have gone,
A	rising are the new dawns,
P	eeping through with sunshine.
P	erhaps because of Stuart.
I	n my dreams once,
N	ow it has become reality,
E	mptiness has gone. I'm
S	tarting my new life now, with
S	tuart, the best thing to ever happen to me!

Victoria Churcher

Mother

Insubstantial goddess that you are
The seasons passed as the
Fluttering calendar recorded
Years that swiftly
Moved without abatement.
What came between was
Memory fixed by a
Face and smile.
Banked by pillows high
Your fingers picking at the sheet
You are transformed.
Intelligence denied, you eke out
Existence like a bad dream.
Day by day.

Angela Cheyne

Remembering You On Father's Day

You were my dad,
Life - it was simple.
I loved you lots,
You loved me too,
Life - it was easy.
Then I grew up,
And you grew old,
Life - it was lovely.
I carried on, but
Your heart stopped,
Life - it was then lonely.

Lynn Edwards

The Golden Wedding Day

Is it really fifty years since Muriel and Peter were wed?

What can we say on this great day, but congratulate
them in every way.

The years have flown, their love has grown, their family
all around them.

These two busy people give pleasure and cheer, to others
who are near and dear.

Let's make two toasts, to our wonderful hosts, as they
travel through life together.

Good health and happiness, and love, may it be theirs
forever.

Isobel Guthrie

Dreamtime

It's the last day of the school year.
Turning around I'm
challenged by a woman
of uncertain time.

The moments before had been filled
with what I could be
or do. Yet she spoke direct to the man
in me. Then I knew
she was a you, altogether an other. She
asserted, 'I can never be known.
Certainly not by you, the predatory self.'

As the dream broke, a once-rich golden array
of tresses streamed about my waking
moment.

There were no eyes,
nothing to touch or much else to see,
only the undefeated will. For,
with a stab of recognition, I saw
you'd won before
and would again. Some
of it all yet might be fun.

So near she seemed to me, so far
she was. The man in me at once knew
I could not ever be
part of either her 'throbbings of eventide'
or a young girl's expectancy.
Woman of uncertain time,
I salute you.

You who cast such a spell, go well.

John K Coleridge

Lady Of Gathered Morning

(For Mum)

Now, sweet lady
Of gathered morning
I come to you here, in
Holy quietness
Special friend still
We sit, together at
This time of three years
Turning. Memories sweet
Like morning chorus sing in
Our hearts and, now,
You have left the arthritis,
The pain, bones cracking
Like winter branches,
You write on my heart
'I am free' and, it's quiet
Now, like an empty church.
Gulls outside call across
The vastness and still
We travel, you bring me to
Light my lady of gathered morning.

George Coombs

Ralf

I love you my grandchild,
I love you so much,
Your face is so perfect,
An angel to touch,
Your nature so sweet,
Angelic you know,
My darling grandchild,
I love you so.

You're growing so fast,
A young man you'll soon be,
I treasure the moment,
You came to me,
You're going to do well just wait and see,
Remember my darling,
You're part of me.

Olive Hudson

The Cowshed

Three years old, cold and tired
up on the cow's back keeping warm.
Yellow milk creamy, steaming,
sloshing rhythmically into the pail.
Warm air, straw smells, cow breath,
heavy and humid and redolent with life.

A tobacco cough and suppressed oath
of a dear man, weary beyond words, of toil.
A life spent scratching and scraping
earning his money wherever he can.
Holes in sweaters, patched knees,
cuffs and collars frayed beyond repair.
And yet a voice lifted in song, shouting
loud defiant praises to a Welsh Deity.

Never one for Sunday church or chapel,
talking directly to his God, man to man.
Complaining of the raw and harsh cards
dealt to the hill farmer above the Mawddach.
Icy cold of too many winters gnarl and bend,
bitter mountain winds gnaw at the joints.
He tilts his cap and smiles at me, lifts me
high into the air to fly above the winter.

I am fearless, shrieking, 'Again, again!'
From that height I see the whole world
laid out for my pleasure and judgement.
I can reach out and pluck its treasures,
all life is there for the taking. My today,
his tomorrow, we face them together.
On his shoulders I ride into the future,
on his devoted bedrock I build my life.

Rona Laycock

Golden Time

A wistful world, a glorious time
To enhance treasures and gifts of thine
This golden age to celebrate your age
A royal princess, now a peaceful queen
Governing our island, however seen
Remember always, keep our island clean
Free from all creeds, that cause horror
Clashes of speech to weld a baton
Guardians of our race and time
Peace, contentment, hot worldly minds,
Rise up, discard those evil lines
From this island's shires, which are kind
To help defend our heritage and self when
Our new age of smiling children
Wave their Union Jacks of peace contentment
'Not rage'

D M Norris

The Welcome Thief

He broke into my life
And stole my heart from me.
A stranger I did not know,
And yet he held the key
To break through my defences,
And steal my very soul.
I gaze at him in wonder,
My baby, one day old.

Sandra Holden

Morag

How should I write to you?
A sister who I never knew.
Whose name was spoken in whispered breath,
whose only feat in life was death.

How should I remember you?
I have a name but nothing else.
I've lit candles, mouthed silent prayers
in Venice, Salzburg and Rome.
But I never dared ask about you
in the one place that mattered:
what would have been our home.

How should I picture you?
There is a photograph I saw when I was fifteen,
of a tiny grave in Aberdeen.
We would have played together
and fought with each other
then made up for birthdays
and missed each other when we went away.

I have no faith to comfort and believe
I know no language with which to grieve
I could have looked up the meaning of *Morag*
but definitions are too abstract
adding nothing to my precious little fact.

With no memories to speak of,
no voice, no laughter, not even a face.
What is left for me to dedicate to you?
Nothing, except a blank space.

Neil Halliday

Bruv

My brother
The good looking alien one
We talk, he does his walk
Head the size of a melon
Comes out with such c**p
God, can he be a plonka at times.

He is my brother
There is only one
Pretty as a picture
Mirror is his best mate
Just really full of p**s and wind

Only joking, bruv.

E A Triggs

Splendour Of The Morn

My lily unfolds
her petals
against my body
as she stretches towards the day
her eyes reflect
the early
light
as lips they part
to play

Tenderly wraps weaves
her stem
around my waist
as her leaves they do enfold
the softness
of her
silkiness
is brushed with skeins
of gold

Séamas M Ó Dálaigh

Daisy

Capture this delicate beauty which fills your sight
with ever so many peaceful shades
that aren't too dull or bright
but set just right.

I know you won't blind me lass
with overshadowed liner
along with cherry red lipstick
to match in with the boisterous makeup
on which I ain't that struck.

The eye of the beholder
is met by every petal so fine
neither falling out nor losing its scent.
Yes o flower in full bloom
for which I feel every desire can make room.

How many of your kind do exist
with a rareness that won't desist?
O one of matchless splendour
who fills the room with every colourful quality of beauty.
Your acts of goodness surround
so as to astound.

O Daisy of the hills,
filled with all naturalness and no pretence.
No disguising of self is needed in your presence
as I feel free -
yes you and me.

Dear one, please don't turn me down
so that in the sun we can both go brown.
A golden relationship will hopefully be in ripe season
with a clear sky so bright
after our lovely night.

A J Lowe

Sonnet To An Aged Love

Shall I compare thee to an ancient tree,
So gnarled your veins are starkly showing,
And girth increases most alarmingly,
Even though your height has sadly ceased its growing,
You're like a tired and weary jumping frog,
In stagnant, weed-filled pool, unheeded, soaking,
That can no longer leap from pond or log,
But still keeps up its never-ending croaking.
Or like an old, disused, warped creaking door,
Its ancient joints in urgent need of healing,
Not so attractive as it was of yore,
Because the fading paint is cracked and slowly peeling.
But, even when time's measured span has spun,
In my warm heart you're still for ever young!

Jack Scrafton

The Lover's Song

If you were a fruit, you would be a fresh lychee,
Hard on the outside but soft within.

If you were a building, how inaccessible
You can be, all doors locked and barred at times.

A piece of furniture and you would be
A warm brown sofa with a cool green throw over.

Only an owl could describe your bird,
But if you were an animal

You would have to be a mule
For how stubborn you can be at times,

And an object? You would have to be
The channel to my heart

Myra Bowen

Patricia

Shall I compare thee to the sun?
You are my morning light.
Or to the effervescent stars?
My fair galaxy at night . . .
bright jewel in my regal crown
fond feather in my cap . . .
Mere words are most inadequate
I dare offer only that
you are my soul, my life, my love,
and what you are to Bill . . .
is simply ill-defined by
incomparable.

W Ballantyne Scott

Small Is Beautiful

(Dedicated to Sylvia - sadly missed, fondly remembered)

Appealingly inquisitive,
She scurries here and there,
Nibbling on her chocolate,
Which is hidden Lord knows where.
The little nest she built for us,
Is comfortable and warm -
Lovingly constructed,
In its every line and form.
Bright-eyed and full of mischief,
She can always make me smile.
She won't give up, she won't give in,
'Cause quitting's not her style.
Her grooming is immaculate:
She always looks her best.
When faced with so much beauty,
Who could care about the rest?
I do my best to keep her safe;
To keep her free from harm,
And she in turn looks after us,
Content within her arms.
She hasn't any whiskers,
And she hasn't any fur,
But I love my little mousekin,
and that's why I married her.

Kevin J Hodge

You

Your smile has cast a shadow on my heart
Your eyes have lit a light in my soul
Your touch has left an imprint on my skin
Your shoulders have carried the burden of my love
Your lips have spoken gently to my ears
Your laughter has infected me with joy
Your voice has whispered words of want
Your hands have held my trembling need
Your breath has made me come alive
Let your feet keep you walking in my world

Sarah Hardy

My Little Devil And Angel

I see you with your red stick dancing around,
Up down, up down
But where is all this energy coming from,
What do you live on?
You pull my hair,
Jump on my tummy, back and legs.
Fast asleep at last.
You look so adorable like an angel.

Parveen K Saini

My Rock

Shall I compare thee to . . ?
a mountain stream -
that floweth with purpose
and cool intent -
to wider outlets
which livelihood deems
essential,
avenues narrow now spent?

Or a mountain tall -
a tower of strength,
which supports with warmth
when chill wind of change
on unachieved prospects
blows cold – arms' length
away peak of fame -
awards out of range?

Shall I compare thee?
I know I shall not -
for thou to me
art a special one, of
unblemished character
with ne'er a blot -
incomparable husband -
My Life - My Love.

Marian Curtis-Jones

Mother

Of treasures,
- To be found,
Few have greater wealth,
Than gold.

But the treasure,
Given to each born of life
Has far greater,
Value and worth.

Than of that,
Which by any,
Can be found
- To own.

Bakewell Burt

Our Time

She left me -
My heart so young,
So vulnerable
She left me -
My heart crying out
For her love
Her guidance.

There had been many threats
Of her leaving,
Nobody took time
To notice, to care;
Then she was gone
My whole life,
My world, my love.

I was lost without her.

My delusion of her love
Left me racked with pain and anguish,
I always thought I'd
Been her favourite.

Then realising I'd been betrayed.

The years have gone by,
I've had new loves
To get me through my life,
But she has been the void
I've been unable to fill.

She's now back in my life,
And I'm desperate to reveal to her
How I've felt all these past long, lonely years;
I need to rest my head
On her breast
And softly whisper,
I love you so much, Mummy.

B J Polhill

Alchemy

(To H from B)

When in my mind I balance all my woes
against the joy that from your brightness springs,
and weigh the heavy weight that with them goes
against the lightness your dear presence brings;
and when in your expressive eyes a tear,
softening laughter, takes compassion's part,
and in the mischief of your voice I hear
the gentle music of your playful heart -
Oh then (strange alchemy!) your lightness turns
the scale of worldly values upside down;
all debts diminish and dull care adjourns
when subject to the sway of your bright crown:
If wealth be marked by weight when it is told,
your lightest glance of love were heaviest gold.

Bernard Brown

A Poem For You

I haven't seen you in years
But, when I wake up each morning
Your name is in my head
Before I wake up properly
Before I open my eyes
How can this still be?

You see, you meant so much to me
You became my life
You became my world
We became a couple
We became one
We became a 'whole'

It came to an end
The walks, holding hands in the sun
It came to an end
Laying on the grass, looking up at the clouds, and laughing
It came to an end
The hugs, the cuddling, the closeness, the warmth
It came to an end
Then you were gone
It was the end.

But when I go to bed and close my eyes
and
Before I go soundly to sleep
I see your face
You are still with me . . . for now.

Nia Michael

Where Were You?

Where were you when I needed you?
Of course, you brought some flowers
then wept in church,
For hours . . .
And hours . . .
And hours.
Was the journey too long
to visit for a day?
Was the journey any shorter,
On this -
my last remaining day?

Jessie Baxter

The Man Who Shot An Albatross

(To David Gillan, second cousin and good friend.
He was truly born with a brassie in his mouth.)

With three generations before him
Hewing out the self-same coal,
Perhaps it was not surprising
That he himself decided
To extend those mining roots
Even more, by also opting
To pursue that fossil ore.

But it was sport that consumed
His prime, and leisure time,
Stroking red leather past fumbling
Slips, or driving an indented
Ball betwixt tee and hole
With practised iron aplomb,
Come hail, rain, or shine.

Even after a long nightshift
Stint below, he and a brace
Of brushers would stop off
At the clubhouse, and against
A backdrop of dawn chorus,
They'd vie for lowest score,
Making birdies, eagles , and occasionally,
Even shooting a rare albatross.

And although he's now passed on,
That royal and ancient sporting man,
He's not really gone too far,
For his ashes have been
Laid to rest just where
Old friends are certain to call,
Deep beneath the bunker sand
Of their course's toughest par.

Andrew Farmer

Love Shared, Love Lost

Deep within my mind there lies
The memory of you that now and then
Reminds me of the life I shared with you
From days when both of us were young and
Lives began to change
There was just the two of us
Then a family we became.

The pleasure of our children growing up
Before our eyes, the laughter and the
Tears we shared, until the day you died.

Deep within my heart there still remains
A tender love for you and the memory
Of the life we shared, one day we will
Renew, but now I write on paper
These memories from the past
To remind me once again of
The love shared and the love I lost.

Eleanor Margaret Brooks

He Cares

*(Joe is 72 years old, and got saved in 2000,
as long as we live, there is time to accept the Lord.
He provided for Joe, he will provide for you all, as well).*

Lord I know you care,
Because you sent us Joe,
In doing this, you showed your double concern
For your children.

You see, we both needed acceptance,
In this confusing world, you had already drawn Joe to you
He was there ready to be part of this family,
You knew his desire, and acknowledged mine.

Your promise of provision fulfilled,
Time and time again, a hug when it was wanted
Help at close hand, Joe didn't understand how much he gave,
Not at first, but he was there, thoughtful,
Giving without any expectation for his self.

I could hardly believe how you answered my silent prayer,
I did not speak it out, but you heard it,
Joe has been such a friend, no demand, or conditions, just willing
He weeps with you, smiles with you.

Jesus, it is no coincidence that you sent Joe,
He is a friend, and he shows deep love for us all,
Unconditional, that goes both ways,
He belongs with us, as we do with him.

Because it was in your plan, and this year
He has grown, given his life, you have filled him,
Opened his mind, allowed him freedom of speech now
He is a renewed man, still an ambassador for you Jesus!
Thank you on behalf of us all, for the gift of Joe.
I know that he feels the same. He cares, because you do.

Louise White

Roydon

Your choice, a different land
    in which to dwell.
Heard the rich and vibrant sounds
    to swell your heart.
Saw from the sky the fall of sun
    suddenly the day to end.
And then the molten moon
    rise up and gleam;
Her time to show a silver sheen.
You smelt the heart of an African soul.
Of all these things, I could not know.
I was not there to share.

My sky was gentle, the seasons rose
    with my heartbeat, one by one,
    in time with another living just begun.
But I was conscious that here,
    another year, another year
    of my English life was passing through.
A time zone that was not of you.

Now the years have passed
    their privileged prime.
In time you came, not late or soon.
But right the moment when we met
    to share the rainbow and low sunset
    close to our hearts; well yes, well yes.
That part of us had stayed.

Janine Vallor

For Nathan

Music of the spirit,
pouring forth like blazing stars
or dripping dew-soft on fragile petals;
burgeoning in mighty chords
or caressing the listener's ear like a soft kiss,
calling forth love, tears
smiles and fears.

Jazz gently swung.
Lyrics sweetly sung.
Polonaise and roundelays,
proudly pounding hymns of praise,
perfections to which we may aspire
and organs thundering in the choir,
players, writers, singers all
and those who hear in solemn hall,
as you weave your vibrant spell
no fears, no timid shyness tell.
Be brave!
Be bold!
And set the jangling spheres ablaze
with music of the heart and mind
to charm us through the dreary days,
and our inmost being find.

David W Lankshear

Just Waiting

(To Percy and many memories)

Percy Tolski was once described as
having 'confused blood' in his veins.
He breathed the air of Paris and walked
streets worn and dusty, in half-light.
He loved the view from Montmarte,
A skyline interesting and impossible to describe.
Sometimes life was un-café and unreal,
Black times washed away with vin blanc.
Sometimes Percy would fall asleep on a bench
Allowing his mind to be bleached white.
In emptiness he would just walk, anywhere
Some ventured to ask - 'What do you do?
Why are you here?' There would be no answer.
Perhaps because he had no answer to give,
He sometimes questioned himself.
What was he doing here - why did he come?
There was a time when he knew of course,
Perhaps he was just waiting!

Clive Cornwall

To G

Gifts such as yours,
Fade not with time,
But grow more precious ever,
The gentleness with which you gave,
Lasts in my heart,
Where I can save,
That tenderness for ever.

Mary Hughes

Adele

I saw you there, it was a surprise, but then I was also lifted,
I watched you as you laughed and talked, unaware of my excitement.
The hum of the room with gentle conversation heightened my senses
I remembered how it used to be and knew we had wrongly fallen
Our knot was untied, but the strings still wafted closely in the breeze.

When you glanced, you smiled, the twinkle was reassuring but wary,
I nodded and the bond was retied in an instant.
How did we fall and why, so much time wasted when our unity
is undenied
The pleasure will be calm and inevitable as will the fear.

Hold out your hand, as mine reaches out, and take it without
compromise
We can walk, side by side for now until sanity
But who knows in our disturbed generation.

John Foster

Mater

*(This poem is dedicated to my best
friend, my mum, Jean Knight)*

And why so difficult
To reward you,
With words, that must
You surely crave?

For this life bestowed
My debt is owed
Yet in word
You remain unpaid

And yet I love thee
So dearly
That if lost, I would
Eternal grieve

For the love that I
Possess for thee,
Time never
Shall retrieve.

Simon Knight

None Other

I have no wealth other than what you give me,
I have no jewels other than your eyes,
I have no treasure other than your pleasure.

I have no sense when you're not near,
I have no touch other than to hold you,
I have no sight other than to see you,
I have no smell other than your perfume.

I have no heart other than to give you,
I have no arms other than to hold you,
I have no hands other than to caress you,
I have no body other than to lay with you
I have no breath other than to warm you

I have no desire other than to please you,
I have no wish other than to be near you,
I have no love other than to give you.

Till tomorrow comes . . .

Michael Ashcroft

Missing You, Julie Savage

*(Friends reunited, Rosebery School 1978
46 names found)*

Remember the mysterious fire in the piano hut?
Miss Morse dividing glacé cherries into four
And the freezing cold swimming pool?
Jane Wykeham

I left school after A levels
And have worked in pensions for 20 years.
Would love to hear from Maria McCarthy.
Stephanie Chipp

I am a maths teacher in Cheam.
Still get together with the old girls.
Anyone heard from Julie Savage? Missing you.
Jane Weller

Dear Jane
Julie died some years ago. Paracetamol overdose.
I miss her too.
Maria McCarthy

Perhaps not. Delete.
Try Primary School.

I still support Arsenal and live in Surrey
Brendan Ruddle
I am running a retro business in Brighton
Kevin O'Doherty

Back to Rosebery.

I still think I am a lot funnier than I am
Rona Hills
Missing you Julie Savage
Maria McCarthy.

Maria Bradley

Mary

Mary devoted herself to her four children,
And her husband named George.
She was always found stuck to the ironing board.
She worked so hard to look after the kids.
She never had time to consider her bids,
Why did she put her husband first?
Because she was his friend - and also his nurse.

She made their clothes, and they all looked divine.
She gave so much time to prepare their tea,
She did all this, and looked after them so well.
She gave all her time to cook and clean.
So just a thank you for being supreme.

E Backham

40 Years Of Love

She was haughty at first, this girl I met
Blue eyes flashing in the bright sun
Which seemed to say 'Do not talk to me!'
But barriers are meant to be broken,
She relents at last.
We dance the night away,
Courting now begins.
Love comes knocking on our hearts
Marriage bells toll the message that
Love has triumphed once again.

40 years on, in this year of
Royal celebrations, our love
Grows stronger and stronger.
And may Mother Nature prolong this
Love for another 40 years.

David G Bromage

The Silent Poem

It lies in a drawer, not forgotten
But unseen,
A lover of yesteryear, no stranger,
Memories to treasure, eyes that
Knew the ocean depths
Of a love so true.

Anniversaries come and go
The years have flown, we were
Young and slim, the smiles within,
Now a photo tucked away
Pain and suffering on your brow
Has taken its toll.

The other you, put away
Gently in a drawer
Knowing you, not forgotten.

Joan Hands

Roger And Jane
Wedding Day 2002

I love you for the smile on your lips
The laughter in your eyes,
The way your hair blows in a summer breeze.
How tears fall like gentle rain from Heaven,
Whenever we watch soap television.
In your heart, how it echoes all around
Sweeter sound even than the skylark or nightingale
Lifting my soul on wings of prayer
Giving thanks.

Roger Brooks

My Special Friend

Thank you Graham,
For helping me through
The years that are left.
For sharing the happy times
Also the sad times.
All these memories we share,
Showing really
How much we care.
Holiday times
Spent with me
My first flight
With you
Across the sea.
Many visits to Cornwall
Just us three.
You, me and our four-legged friend.
These memories I treasure,
And will to the end.
Thank you
My special friend.

Patricia M Farbrother

A Symphony In Grey

(Dedicated to the memory of Miss Minie)

Dark grey clouds roll
  across the horizon
  like a rumbling timpani.
Floating aloft,
  dove grey clouds
  with the sweet of violins.
Higher blue grey clouds
  soar to the swell
  of the wood winds.
All blend into a
  thundering climax.

The rumble continues
  as the storm
  moves across the land.
A patch of bright blue
  appears, the sky clears
  the air is freshened.
As the fury
  of the storm subsides,
  the gloom of a
  November sky is
a symphony in grey.

M E Vanderwulp

A Poem For Nan

When I was a child
Headstrong and wild
I lived next door to my nan
Caring and sweet
Tiny, petite
Undoubtedly head of the clan.

Six children she bore
And she made sure
They grew up honest and true
Each one possessed
The very best
Possessions that Nan could accrue.

She always had time
To tell us a rhyme
Or maybe a story or two
Never a harsh word
That I ever heard
But praise was quick when due.

Her home-made bakes
The pies and the cakes
Were the envy of the neighbourhood
Trips to the sea
With picnics for tea
I'd return to those days if I could.

And now that she's died
Something's missing inside
My rock that I cannot replace
But the memories remain
Locked deep in my brain
Those that time will never erase.

Marilyn Wellman

Thank You Jesus

Lord, I want to lift You on high
for all that You've done for me,
I want to exalt Your name to the heavens,
for You have set me free,
washing me free from sin,
making me a new person,
all the glory is Yours, again and again.
Thank You for Your faithfulness,
Your mercy and love,
for stretching out Your hand to me,
for always being my God,
for showering Your blessings,
like golden drops of rain,
for pouring out Jesus' blood,
for giving me Heaven to gain,
for walking close in times of sorrow,
for rejoicing for my every tomorrow,
for being You in Your awesome way,
for declaring God's glory, Holy Spirit, every day,
for making a pure heart,
from that which was rotten,
for picking me out,
so that I would not be forgotten,
for choosing a plan,
before I was even conceived,
for giving me a life, that I have received,
reverently, thankfully and joyfully to You
I shall give You all praises,
for all praises are due,
to the king of kings,
and the Lord of Lords,
to the bright morning star and Son of God,
who took my place on a blood-stained cross,

so that not one battle
in my life would ever be lost,
from the depths of my heart
I shout Hallelujah to You
for You have enabled me to be,
to be as new.

Samantha Drewry

What Are Mams And Dads?

*(God bless you both and thank you so much
Mam and Dad, for my life)*

Mams and dads are those two very special
people in our lives, and having enough love
in each other brought forth our existence.
Showing so much love for us and guiding us through life.
They are always there for us, no matter what happens in our lives.
They share all of our joys, and sorrows and
do it for us because they love us.
They are always there in our thoughts
throughout every day in our lives because,
as their children, we love them with all of our hearts.
They are the very meaning to our lives, and
through this meaning all things are possible.
Even when they are no longer with us, their love
still lives in us and will always live in us forever.
They provide us with all of our most memorable
and happy times in our lives and today as each day
passes, I remember them so, with a loving but aching heart.

F J Lawton

The Package

(For Rob)

He says my train of thought
Is almost pure James Joyce,
Ramblings of a madman,
When it's just a vocal form.
His whole self is professionally odd
Never ceasing to amaze
Dumbfound by his profession's existence
Life's a comedy,
And you're playing the straight role
Where 'people are a test'
Unbelievable at times
A brilliant being
Of slacker genius,
Where a dented empty beer can
Or cardboard pipe will suffice
For its purpose
Red lights, records and a little enhancement
Smoking in a surround-sound living room
Now linked up
Accessed to the world
Plugged in, reaching out
With spontaneous planned bouts of energy
Clicking into work mode,
Then back to the couch
For a fixed wired expression
Comforted by wine, friends and that special one.

Kevin Rolfe

Just One More Spoonful

This is the tale of Annaliese, who wouldn't eat her ham or cheese,
And turned quite pale when given lamb, or chicken pie or
strawberry jam.
Screwed up her nose at stew or roast . . . the only thing she ate
was toast!
Her dog was well pleased, so it's said, watching from his smelly bed,
Knowing if he cared to wait, he'd get that food from off her plate!
His coat grew glossy, his tummy fat, gobbling this and scoffing that!
I've heard one day she had a moan, when her dog mistook her for
a bone
And buried her in the compost heap - when really she was just asleep!
When coming home, she found no more she'd have to open up the
door,
Instead she'd slither through the keyhole, like a slug or worm
or beanpole.
And as she wouldn't eat her dinner, she just got thinner and
thinner and
Thinner!
One day when running from the rain, she found herself washed down
a drain,
And when winds blew with all their might, some small boys flew her
like a kite!
She couldn't swim or trampoline, or ride the horse, she was so lean.
Her hair dropped out, she couldn't poo, her mother cried
'What can I do? Why can't she be like other folk? This faddiness is
past a joke!'
A keeper working at the zoo, thought what he saw could not be true -
'A stick insect is loose,' said he, 'or is it just a mutant flea?'
And thinking her a scrawny louse, he caged her in the Insect House!
Folk peered into the cage and said, 'What thing is that, curled in
its bed?
It has no feathers, scales or fur, it doesn't squeak, or bark or purr.
It's pretty bony, doesn't fly, all it does is sit and cry!'

She curled up in a corner where she dreamed of apple, orange, pear,
And all that food she'd said she'd hate, and left congealing on her
plate.
Her mother said 'Oh, that's no flea. That skinny child belongs to me,
I'll take her home now, if you please, and see she eats her ham
and cheese.'
The moral of this tale, it's true, is that this story, could be you!
So eat your food up every day. You'll be the best at work and play!

Yvonne Lane

A Mother's Recipe

What's a mother made of?
What makes her all soft and sweet?
What's the taste of loveliness that makes you feel complete?

There's a hint of sharpness -
Just enough to keep . . .
Your heart and mind instructed
On the right paths for your feet

That recipe - so perfect
Made by the master baker
Our dear Heavenly Father - the very essence of a mother.

These ingredients all well balanced out
Its taste you'll want more and more
Then at night before you go to sleep
You'll thank you Father in Heaven!

Isabel Morgan

I Miss You

Your touch was like
A fond memory
That drifted past my ears
As the wind was whispering
The pictures to my head.

Your touch was like a flower in bloom;
While under the moon -
Light, strong enough
To reveal the shining wet
Dew, caught in a web.

Your touch like warm stone;
Strong in the fist
That's keeping it warm,
Away from all harm
When all's been done and said.

You touch like a dream,
That all my lives had seen,
And they thank you
For the love
I think was meant for me.

Lydia Moore

For Janet

(With all my love. Thank you for being there).

My daughter, my best friend.
All through life's journey
you have been there for me.
My friend and confidante.

Slender and elfin of feature
yet strong and wise of soul.
You keep me safely
anchored to the ground
when my spirit starts to roam.

Your wisdom and your healing touch
have oft been my salvation.
You're always there to lend a hand
in all life's tribulations.

My daughter, my best friend.
An angel in training,
An angel in disguise.

Brigitta D'Arcy

Farewell Princess

Farewell beautiful princess,
May flights of angels
Carry thee to thy rest,
Though it is still impossible
To believe that you have gone
From us forever.

No longer shall we see
Your vision bestride the world,
Bringing hope
Friend of the sick and injured,
Beacon of the good causes,
Comforter to the dying,
Lost to us, and all the world,
Who met with kings, queens and presidents,
And loved children.

Vision of loveliness, who dazzled,
And lit up the world stage
In a bright light,
Caring mother of fine boys,
Loving and compassionate,
Joyous and playful,
You leave behind a legacy,
To follow in your good deeds,
To carry on.

Terry Daley

A Daughter

Yes, I have a
Special person,
My daughter.
She was a
Life saver
Through death,
It gave me
Time to catch
My breath.

Barbara Brown

Deep And Darker Brown

Shut in my room, engrossed in my work,
suddenly the doorbell rang, disturbing the Saturday afternoon
and uninvitedly snapping my train of thought.

I knew no one in the neighbourhood
who would intrude the hallowed hours.
Cross, I stopped, put down my pen
went to the door and pulled it open;
stunned with shock, I couldn't move -
on the doorstep stood my dream.

Nine long years since last we met,
despite our lives so far apart, nothing had changed.
No speck of grey aged the gold of the flowing hair;
unlined and fresh the sunburned face; the ever winning
melting smile; the flowered blouse and flaring jeans
trimmed a figure slim as ever; but, above all, the deep brown eyes
just looked and said in silence, wonderful, nothing has changed.
No time for talk, just superficials as others in the car outside
gave a friendly wave.

How she knew and found me, a miracle indeed: that she wanted
to -
I don't know the superlative of miraculous, but this was it all right.
The intensely dark deep brown, deeper eyes then said
It's time to go, but in their saying was great sadness.

After nine long years of dreaming, it would not be surprising
if the subject itself had faded just a little bit.
But God in His great wisdom had worked a little miracle on that
Saturday afternoon - the flower was still in perfect bloom.

My work was hard; the message of the dark, dark eyes was harder
still
- strangely posed on a Saturday afternoon;
my only comfort was to know that after nine long years,
the reality was, in very truth, so much, much better
than in my dreaming.

Edward Fursdon

To Gina

I looked at you today and thought, my God
We've had fun and we've had some stormy weather.
I'll tell you something that I think's quite odd
About the life we've lived these years together:
I haven't been an ordinary dad,
Nor have you been the usual sort of mother.
But still through all the good times and the bad
At least we've always talked to one another.
Our children can't say that they've been ignored;
We've tried not to indulge them or to flatter.
Nor have they had much reason to be bored,
Or been starved of affection for that matter.
I guess that I must love you in my way,
Not only now, but always, every day.

Chris Gutteridge

My Dad, My Hero

While I was in Australia,
My dear dad passed away.
No one will ever know
How sad I am,
Not being with him on that day.
For four years he had Parkinson's,
And he was very ill,
But the end came suddenly
I can't believe it still.
I stood upon the sea shore,
On a beach so far away.
I let balloons up in the sky
And watched them fly away,
I hoped they would be carried
On a cloud to Heaven above,
And be delivered by an angel
To my dad, with all my love.

I often think about him
When I am all alone,
All the things he did for me
Since the day that I was born.
We didn't have much money
But our house was filled with love,
Dad made us wonderful toys
With collected bits of wood.
Happy times to remember
As I walk life's tough highway,
I feel Dad walk beside me
With each step I take each day.
So sleep peacefully Dad,
You have earned your rest,
I just want you to know
You simply were the best.

Pat Munzer

Diana

D iamond of perfect beauty and lustre, heart of gold
I mpregnated with deep love and compassion
A ngel adored and admired by every nation
N aturally loving and kind to the sick, down-trodden, rejected;
A ll these things and much, much more.

The queen of all hearts, throughout the world,
Let us hold in our hearts and remember her love and work;
By following her shining example of . . .

Showing great kindness, tolerance and love to our fellow beings
As Diana did let us also cast a bright light where dark shadows lurk;
Let her spirit live on in our memories and hearts;
By casting out instruments of war, greed, animosity and power
As Diana is at peace, let the world be also
In the image of her selfless love and devotion.

Frederica Greenway

Man Of Years

Hands that held
a rifle at war
are holding now a stick.

Eyes that shone
with love and passion,
dim with passing days.

Lips that fed
on his mother's breast,
tremble with silent thought.

Voice of command
is now a whisper,
of days gone by.

When you see
that man of years,
oh please do remember.

Marshal Green

The Death Of Princess Margaret

The death of Princess Margaret
Took my mind back many years ago
When I was a guest
At the staff ball in Buckingham Palace.
The whole night became a dream
A gold and white ballroom
With the royal family attending.
Our late king was there
Along with the Queen Mother
And the two princesses.
To me, fresh from the WRNS
And coupons still around
The whole night was magical.
Princess Elizabeth, then
Looked to me, what she became:
'Our wonderful Queen'.
Regal and beautiful
But Margaret was as her name
Implied
'A Princess'
Dainty, delightful, charming.
Each year I attended those parties
I wondered who she would look like
She could have been a rival
To any of the film stars
Of the day.
That's how I shall remember her.
Such a long time ago.

J Nicoll

Margaret Rose

*(I wrote this when Princess Margaret Rose was getting a lot of
bad publicity which I thought very unfair. Suffering 'migraine' all
my life I knew what she was going through)*

No fairer rose has graced
this queenly land,
cursed be the pointed finger -
the stone-casters,
the tongues that prattle
do not understand -
nor try to:
who thrive on defamation
until saliva drips from
their overted mouths.
Wilt not this fair rose
who carries on graciously,
best she can, her royal duties
where they demand,
leaving enigmatic questioners
far behind, unanswerable,
because they would not understand:
the overstrain - the energetic
feeling of well-being suddenly
turns to pain, yet still her
duties tries best to perform.
Only those prone to similar distress
are one with fair Margaret
our Royal Patroness.

Isabella F Veitch

A Beautiful Lady

Princess Margaret Rose died today
On the 9th February 2002,
At half-past six she closed her eyes
And quietly slipped away
A beautiful lady, a real princess
Her ashes will be laid to rest near her father
It is where she wanted to be.
She will be sadly missed by her children
And all the people she knew
And by our queen her sister
Rest in peace without any pain.

Margaret Stumpp

Our English Rose

She blossomed, our Princess Margaret Rose,
A favourite daughter, of our English Isle.
Her steel blue eyes brightly
Highlighting her lovely smile.
That touch of velvet to her completion,
Her full rose petal lips, glossed,
Your dress, the ultimate perfection.
Your life, was full and like any ones
Troubled and fraught,
You moved away from strife,
Your island retreat bought.
We saw you grow to maturity,
With style, and love, and royal grace.
When you came back home from Mustique,
We saw the pain upon your royal face.
You came back to love,
Care and opened carriage doors,
Sadly you came back home to die.

Remembering you;
Margaret our English Rose.

Susan Carole Roberts

Christine

Christine my mother
She was born 21st June 1957
She was indeed a fine loving mother
Christine my mother
I love and loved my mother
We had some good times
We had some good laughs
She was always pleasant and polite
She was indeed a mother amongst the best
She was indeed beautiful
She loved flowers, carnations her favourite
She also loved Elvis Presley,
She liked too Shakin' Stevens, Jim Reeves,
Def Lepard's Joe Elliott
They would have liked her too
If they would have met
She did meet once cricketer Alan Lamb
Also Benny from the original cast
Of the programme Crossroads.
She was chuffed
Well my mother, a princess now in heaven
Loved by many she was
Always now in my thoughts
Christine my mother
She is now sadly missed by many
But I'll always love her
She's always in my heart
She's always in my thoughts
She died 11th February 1991
When I was 13
Now in heaven
Loved and sadly missed
Christine my mother.

Michelle Knight

Fly Like A Bird

Flight without wings, head thrust forward,
arms back, feet splayed,
on a beak of skis to tongue the snow . . .

I, a feather from his nest,
float down with him,
knowing the lightness of birds,
flying behind him in the camera's wake,
with Olympian hopes, on a snowy slope,
sharp air tingling, sun glinting,
above the gaping fish-mouths of crowds below.
In a soaring moment - free of gravity,
aloof, aloft, above it all,
elation rises with elevation.

Torso-straightening from an acute angle,
he lands the jump, and glides,
eagle-glancing up to see his score.
He has taken me to heights of glory,
this slender birdling plunged from an eyrie,
swooping for a disc
to become a gold throat.

Marian Reid

Princess Diana (1961-1997)

(The life of Diana, Princess of Wales is now legendary, and could be compared with the famous love saga of 'willow pattern' china. Her blue-blood love story enduring for generations to come)

A grim fairytale
of the tortured
queen of hearts;
captive within
palace walls.
Made her escape
into a goldfish
bowl; where she
kissed many frogs
in search of her
true prince.
Waving among crowds,
and media coverage,
her royal affairs
caught public
imagination
and speculation,
until her story
closed; when the fair
rose faded, before
September shadows
cast a spell.
Though her spirit
dwells; a bluebird,
in every willow pattern.

Josie May Hodges

A Soul Concern

Most thoughts, of famous ones,
would be of hear-say, so why say,
that he - she was all those wondrous,
things, for we shall return to dust,
with little to boast about,
a soul to travel to
where heart and spirit
sought to dwell.

Examples of excellence
will inspire the willing,
in Christ like way,
sparkling in humbleness,
with little to fear of death,
whatever walk of life we come.

Our human value has its purpose,
our trials and tribulations,
differ from each other,
our statues may have its place on Earth,
to flaunt or enrich,
tis God who knows us as no other,
with a just reward.

Oh human kind,
stop think and pray,
the safest place to be
to wrestle with much
that interferes
in soul enrichment.

Rachel Taylor

Dear Sister

When you were born
I looked upon your face
So fair you stole my heart
For you were so rare.

You were just like a rose
Petal soft was your skin
You stole all our hearts
With your cute little ways.

With you I spent some happy days
Playing hide and seek, happy bygone days
As young ladies we had such fun
Playing at grown-ups and making fun.

Best of all you grew up to be a mum
Your children loved you for you made up games for everyone
You had so much love for everyone
We all have fond memories of you
You were our darling precious one.

M Ackroyd

Mum

(Words will never be enough to show our love for you, but I know you loved reading my poems so here's one for you)

A great, great person,
Full of love for everyone,
The best mum we could have hoped for,
The only one we'd ever want,
The best wife Jim could have hoped for,
The only one he'd ever want,
So good,
She was like a second mum to many,
Caring for others more than herself,
An emotional person granted,
Only because she cared so much,
Any way she could, she would,
A cup of coffee the best,
A held hand, a big cuddle,
Always willing to give,
Always there in moments of need,
A happy caring person,
This is my memory,
The years of pain now gone,
A relaxing life she now leads,
Up there with Grandad and Penny,
Knowing our every thought,
Knowing how much we loved her,
Life will continue,
For that is what she'd want,
We'll do our best for you now Mum,
Your body may have died,
But Carol Elizabeth Stirk,
A loving mum and wife,
Will never die.

Neil Stirk

Theresa - A Memory

(Thornwick Bay, Flamborough, 1967)

We met beneath a holiday moon, arranged to meet next day at noon.
We walked and talked, we combed the beach, skipped
breaking waves, keeping just out of reach.
We watched the seabirds overhead, I remember,
your skirt was a fiery red.
And all the world was just a game, and each of us knew,
we felt the same.

Time stood still, at least, we thought, the ways of love,
each other we taught.
The fleetest touch, a feather-light kiss, holding hands in youthful bliss.
Walking together, the world shut outside, for what
we felt was deep inside.
I was 14, so were you, the sun shone bright, the sky was blue.

And as evening stretched into the night, so the moon cast its glow
on our teenage delight.
But with the coming of each new day, so grew shorter our holiday stay.
Until the time came, when we had to part, and we both felt a deep
wrenching, a pull in the heart.
We said a tearful last goodbye, I tenderly kissed each red rimmed eye.

Would we ever meet again? We thought we would, but that was then.
I said goodbye, waved as you left, and my youthful heart
was broken, bereft.
And now the holiday was done, no more evenings with you,
no more walks in the sun.
Home once more, back to daily existence, yet your memory re-
mained with dogged persistence.
Time marches on, time we must live, we love and we suffer,
we take and we give.
Yet, somewhere inside, there's a part of my heart, that seems to
remember when it all seemed to start.

So many years have passed and yet, I remember you still,
and the day we met.
Theresa, Theresa, I still remember your name, do you remember
me too, my heart's first true flame?

Brian L Porter

Alexandra

A little girl
A tiny surprise
Dark hair and blue eyes
A wriggling joy
Sings a simple song
A cuddle? A feed?
A complex world
Has simple needs
Like springtime trees
Just ask for leaves
And flowers
Just want to bloom
And birds are singing
A child's song
Alexandra!
And peacefully you sleep
Innocence that once was mine
Is now forever to keep.

A Moore

Dad

A father is someone you look up to, however tall you grow.

To guide you through the path of life, to teach you all
                                        you need to know.

To him you turn in times of fear, in his smile you seem to grow.

From that innocent girl of yesterday, to the young
                                        woman he now knows.

Laura O'Rourke

Someone Much Loved

The sad passing of the Princess Royal
has touched many hearts far and wide.
As in life her popularity
had enchanted many lives.

Margaret was the people's princess
an ambassador in her day.
The free spirit of the royals
much loved by everyone.

Those that had know the princess
were touched by her many charms.
Have felt the pain and sorrow
at the sad passing of her life.

A beautiful person was taken
Sorrow as the rose fades.
In our hearts her memory dwells
That's left the world to mourn.

A radiant life now sadly gone
extinguished like a flickering flame
has left a shallow void.
A life that cannot be replaced.
The sad demise of the Princess Royal.

Burgess J Barrow

Mei Tak

You were always sad, irritating, easily got upset . . .
I guess you were sick already.
Maybe you did not have good food.
Maybe there were worms in your stomach
burning up all your energy.

By the time
you were extremely sick
you were sent to the hospital
and you died not long later.

For your funeral
there was nobody from our family had attended.
Our father was so upset and got drunk.
Our mother was still in the hospital
having a younger sister or brother.

Where was your body?
Who took care of it in the end?
I don't even know where is your tomb.
Not even the place for your ash!

It's very, very sad
to think of your life
short and sad
with not much fun and dignity . . .

When I followed the two elder sisters
to burn the paper money and stuff for you in the street
I came home walking up and down the stairs
and my sister scolded at me that I should pay more
                                        respect than having fun.
I am sorry

Mei Yuk Wong

Dunkirk - The Final Tribute

*(60 years have passed since the Normandy/Dunkirk crossing.
Veterans have decided not to celebrate in so grand a style, be-
cause of the ages of the men, but to make individual trips to
Dunkirk till they are no longer able)*

Little ships at bay, listen to what they say
Veterans of long gone war returned to Dunkirk today
From Britain's welcoming shores, commemorating
The bravery of four hundred thousand soldiering men
Who showed great courage then.

With inborn determination and pride in their country,
Confidence in their leaders, who like Churchill helped
make Britain 'Great'
Rulers of might and steel - in full command!
They soldiered on into the night in defence of what is good, is right
Then came the timely call to retreat,
Strength in wane, but God renewed that strength
With just minutes to spare, they lined the shores of Dunkirk.

Fleeing silently in disciplined hordes
To little ships anxiously lining the shore.
Poignant memories of the hour that herald dawn
Captured in this final tribute, from grateful men.
Humble and unassuming men who felt 'it was the call of duty'.
Who spoke with pride of a job 'well done'
And who now show gratitude to those who gave their lives,
Stayed behind to proudly serve their country to the end
One last stand to rid the world of Hitler's tyranny.

For though 60 years have gone past, recalling days of tiredness
And hope in reaching Britain's friendly shores.
Thought of anxiously awaiting family and of friends,
Of those who stood in their defence, gave up their
lives in hail of German shells.
Yet as they celebrate, more plans were made today
To continue coming to this shore to honour those
brave comrades who are no more.

A Yap-Morris

Smile

I like for you
To smile for me.
Though many a chair
Is vacant you see.
In my dreams
I see you smile
Whenever the stars
Fade from the sky.

Helen Owen

Mary's Love

If you want to know what love is really like
Then watch her go down to the garden
Early while all else sleeps
To seek her resurrected Lord.

Today the garden is her home
The Lord, her friends,
Her loved ones, her animals,
Her plants, to whom love is given
In abundance, unconditionally.

Greater love has no woman
In that she lays down her life for her friends.

Still she washes the feet of the Master with her tears
And dries them with her hair.

John Crowe

Just An Ordinary Afternoon

*(Miss Lambert passed away one month before her 101st birthday.
Now she is with the young men who fell 80 years ago. I do wonder if they are flying with the angels?)*

Two gentle knocks at my door and in they come smiling.
'Time for a change Miss Lambert, we thought you would like to sit
And watch the people walking by on the promenade
And look at the ships across the sea.'
'I am afraid we will have to use the hoist.
I know it is uncomfortable. We will be as quick as we can.'
Uncomfortable is not the word I would use, more like a straight jacket.
'We are just going to gently swing you over the bed,' they said.
Well, fine if you like swinging on a high trapeze.
'Safe and sound in your chair, now that was not too bad was it?'
That is what they think, how can they know what it is like
to have useless legs?
One girls stays and fusses around me, putting my stockings and
slippers on and a nice warm blanket on my legs.
'You are right in the sunlight and now you can enjoy the sea.
What more could you want? See you again soon.'
What more could I want? Well, I can remember the sun in my face,
The wind on my back, cycling along narrow lanes, wild flowers,
Nodding from every hedgerow and a large brown bag full of post.
Yes I was sixteen and a post mistress in a small village.
The year was 1916. The hardest part of the job was delivering the
brown envelopes marked private and confidential.
The look upon the women's faces as I handed them the letters.
The messages were brief and controlled.
'I am sorry to inform you that your son has fallen at Somme.'
So many of our brave young men were killed fighting for peace.
'Hello Miss Lambert, were you day dreaming?
It will soon be time for tea.'

She returned with my tea, popped the small spoon into my mouth
And chatted to me about how wonderful it would be
when we get to Heaven.
She said 'You will be able to walk and dance and maybe fly
with the angels.'
I smile and think that would be nice.

Deborah Grimwade

Elizabeth Our Queen

When my eyes first perceived
Elizabeth our queen
I felt in awe and wonderment, the moment was surreal
As I grew older I thought that this would pass
On viewing yet again, the feeling I know will last
Proud to be British
Grateful for our queen
Who has carried out her duties with dignity so serene
Through trials and tribulations
Like the rest of mortal man
Never has she faltered
From her destined plan
Never veered from duty
Never had a choice
Unlike her subjects
Not even a voice
Just done what is expected
Not the current vain
Elizabeth our noble queen
Long may she reign.

Wendy Le Maitre

Untitled

Back in '77 I was 10 or 11?
My little school, the honour we gained
Princess Anne came to visit.
I shook her hand,
Said 'How do you do ma'am?' She smiled!
I'm now 34,
Can't see the Queen at my door,
God bless ma'am, I'm with you in spirit.

Colin Drummond

Peter

To some people
    You would appear stupid,
For you are not like the rest of us.
    You cannot speak -
At least not with your mouth.
But you can speak
    With your eyes.
You have learnt to adapt and use your eyes
    To say what you want.
We cannot all understand you;
Only those who care for you -
    Who love you.
We know how your eyes speak.
They have learnt to say 'Yes' and 'No'
As you move your eyes in a certain direction.

Why were you born with such a handicap?
    Life is so unfair,
That you were disadvantaged
    From the start.
A pitiful sight to most of us,
Slumped upon a bean bag,
Stiff and unable to move yourself,
Grunting words that are unintelligible.
Dribbling salvia from a distorted face.
But filled with compassion,
I want to care for you.
We who have health
    And life ahead
Do not always have the privilege
Of meeting such special children.

Your eyes communicate
More than a thousand words could,
And you probably see things
That most of us would miss.
You cannot speak, but
Your laughter fills the room
     With joy.
Despite all,
     You can laugh at life.
     You are a special child.

Your days with us may not be many,
But you can teach us -
We can learn from you
That each one of us has something to offer -
     However small.
No one is useless.
Whatever our handicap is in life
God can still use us.
We can learn to laugh again.

We are all God's special children.
Each one important,
     Valuable.
     Loved by Him,
     Special.

Sue Trickey

The Soldiers Of The Queen

We're the soldiers, we're the soldiers,
We're the soldiers of the queen,
We fight by her banners, in war and in peace,
Oh, we're the soldiers, we're the soldiers,
We're the soldiers of the queen,
We fight by her in peace or war.
In peacetime we fight for the love of fair beauty,
In battle we fight with a grim sense of duty,
But always with cheerful, cheerful smiles,
For though the soldiers, though the soldiers,
Though the soldiers of the queen,
Yet we try to fight our battles in peace,
And if any should ask you who we are
Why then you'll point to every man,
Every Englishman who loves his queen,
Queen of court or village green,
For we're the soldiers, we're the soldiers
Of many fair queens,
And Elizabeth, queen of all greens,
Oh, we're the soldiers, we're the soldiers,
We're the soldiers of the queen,
We fight by her even in happiest peace,
We dance and we sing,
We're fond of a fling,
Our thoughts they stream widely and high,
And soaring in planes, the fruit of our inventive brains
We try to scale queenhood's, reach queenhood's far sky,
We're the soldiers of the queen in a great jubilee,
A really joyous jubilee.

Tony Dixon

Our Grandchildren

1979 -
We have a little grandson,
Oh! So precious and so dear,
Just one year old, and lively,
As lively as can be,
He loves to open cupboards,
And longs to find a key.

His little sister loves him,
She is nearly four,
She also is a treasure, and
We couldn't love them more.
She loves to paint and colour
Shells and pictures by the score.

They are the dearest children,
That anyone could have,
They have the best of mothers,
And the greatest of dads.
Of course we may be biased,
Being grandma and grandad.

2002 -
Many years have passed,
Since first I penned these words.
Grandad has gone to glory
The children both grown up,
With another lovely brother.
All have done well in many ways.
But I still love them oh so much,
And give my God all the praise.

Ruth Baker

A Tribute To Kevin . . .

An amazing man, that words cannot enough describe,
  Only words that come so close, no other can deny.

Dedicated, and committed, were his fighting beliefs,
  The potential to reach the sky.

Determined and motivated, were unbelievably high.
  Hardworking, courageous, and strong he was.

That brought tears to our eyes,
  Fighting the battle that enlightened us.

Respect and faith, we felt for Kevin,
  Truly an inspiration, that we envy.

A gifted well-loved individual,
  And everyone agrees.

To Kevin, we will never forget you,
  Even though you are not here, you will always be in our hearts.

Angela Tsang

My Two Angels Of Beauty

I have an angel of beauty
Walking close by my side
I have an angel of beauty
And she's my tender loving bride
Dear Carol.

Her angel eyes sparkle brighter
Than the stars at night
Her angel's bright smile
Is so soft, warm and wide
And her slender angel's body
Always feels so warm and tender
Every time I hold her closer and closer to me.

So thank you dear Lord above
For an angel of beauty to love
And for another sweet little angel
Who's just popped her head
Into my life
And she's my little daughter Wendy
Who's only fifteen months old.

Donald John Tye

To Elizabeth From Her Grandmother

We all know the maiden of sweet 17
        Who swears she's never been kissed.
With lips rosy red and skin like a peach
The fullness of life she's longing to reach.

The future is calling to one such as you,
        The whole world lies at your feet
Whatever life brings to you through all your years
May courage and love dispel all your fears.

As you travel along through life's busy ways
        Through days sometimes happy or sad
Remember your friends and your family too
Who love you for ever because you are you.

From baby to toddler and then days at school
        We've seen every part of your life.
17 years filled with anticipation
Of days filled with hope and great expectations.

Passing along through life's myriad ways
Many gifts you will gather and treasure.
But the greatest of these, the love in your heart
Will give joy to your life beyond measure.

On life's busy highway whomever you meet
        Be friendly and give them a smile.
For the smile that you give may bring warmth and hope
To someone whose life has been sad for a while.

A brief glimpse of hope that the sun does still shine
        Through the smile that you gave on your way.
        The sadness dispelled by the gift of a smile,
                Like sun after rain -
        Your smile made their day.

B E

You Mean The World To Me

(Dedicated to Alex, the man who completes me)

You mean the world to me
You have changed my life
In so many ways
You have made me so happy
You make me feel so lucky
Every single day
You mean the world to me.

You mean the world to me
You are a wonderful,
Special, kind person
You inspire me to be all I can
To live life to the full
To have fun
And I mean it,
You mean the world to me.

Lindsey Hood

SUBMISSIONS INVITED
SOMETHING FOR EVERYONE

POETRY NOW 2003 - Any subject,
any style, any time.

WOMENSWORDS 2003 - Strictly women, have
your say the female way!

STRONGWORDS 2003 - Warning!
Age restriction, must be between 16-24,
opinionated and have strong views.
(Not for the faint-hearted)

All poems no longer than 30 lines.
Always welcome! No fee!
Cash Prizes to be won!

Mark your envelope (eg *Poetry Now*) ***2003***
Send to:
Forward Press Ltd
Remus House, Coltsfoot Drive,
Peterborough, PE2 9JX

OVER £10,000 POETRY PRIZES
TO BE WON!

Judging will take place in October 2003